Comfort Food

Salisbury Steaks with Mushroom-Wine Sauce

1 pound ground beef sirloin

¾ teaspoon garlic salt or seasoned salt

¼ teaspoon black pepper

2 tablespoons butter

1 package (8 ounces) sliced button mushrooms *or* 2 packages (4 ounces each) sliced exotic mushrooms

2 tablespoons sweet vermouth or ruby port wine

1 jar (12 ounces) *or* 1 can (10½ ounces) beef gravy

1. Heat large heavy nonstick skillet over medium-high heat 3 minutes or until hot.* Meanwhile, combine ground sirloin, garlic salt and pepper; mix well. Shape mixture into four ¼-inch-thick oval patties.

2. Place patties in skillet as they are formed; cook 3 minutes per side or until browned. Transfer to plate. Pour off drippings.

3. Melt butter in skillet; add mushrooms. Cook and stir 2 minutes. Add vermouth; cook 1 minute. Add gravy; mix well.

4. Return patties to skillet; simmer uncovered over medium heat 2 minutes for medium or until desired doneness, turning meat and stirring sauce.   *Makes 4 servings*

If pan is not heavy, use medium heat.

Note: For a special touch, sprinkle cooked steaks with chopped fresh parsley or chives.

Prep and Cook Time: 20 minutes

Double-Baked Potatoes

3 large baking potatoes
4 tablespoons milk, warmed
1 cup (4 ounces) shredded Cheddar cheese
¾ cup corn
½ teaspoon chili powder
1 tablespoon finely chopped fresh oregano *or* 1 teaspoon
   dried oregano leaves
   Nonstick cooking spray
1 cup chopped onion
½ to 1 cup chopped poblano peppers*
3 cloves garlic, minced
½ teaspoon salt
¼ teaspoon black pepper
3 tablespoons chopped fresh cilantro

Poblano peppers can sting and irritate the skin; wear rubber gloves when handling peppers and do not touch eyes. Wash hands after handling peppers.

1. Preheat oven to 400°F. Scrub potatoes under running water with soft vegetable brush; rinse. Pierce each potato with fork. Wrap each potato in foil. Bake about 1 hour or until fork-tender. Remove potatoes; cool slightly. *Reduce oven temperature to 350°F.*

2. Cut potatoes in half lengthwise; scoop out insides, being careful not to tear shells. Set shells aside. Beat potatoes in large bowl with electric mixer until coarsely mashed. Add milk; beat until smooth. Stir in cheese, corn, chili powder and oregano. Set aside.

3. Spray medium skillet with cooking spray. Add onion, poblano peppers and garlic; cook and stir 5 to 8 minutes or until tender. Stir in salt and black pepper.

4. Spoon potato mixture into reserved potato shells. Sprinkle with onion mixture. Place stuffed potatoes in small baking pan. Bake 20 to 30 minutes or until heated through. Sprinkle with cilantro.

Makes 6 servings

Velveeta® Ultimate Macaroni & Cheese

2 cups (8 ounces) elbow macaroni, uncooked
1 pound (16 ounces) VELVEETA® Pasteurized prepared
    Cheese Product, cut up
½ cup milk
    Dash pepper

1. Cook macaroni as directed on package; drain well. Return to same pan.

2. Add VELVEETA, milk and pepper to same pan. Stir on low heat until VELVEETA is melted. Serve immediately.

Makes 4 to 6 servings

Easy Pineapple Slaw

1 can (15¼ ounces) DEL MONTE® Pineapple Tidbits
    In Its Own Juice
⅓ cup mayonnaise
2 tablespoons vinegar
6 cups coleslaw mix or shredded cabbage

1. Drain pineapple, reserving 3 tablespoons juice.

2. Combine reserved juice, mayonnaise and vinegar; toss with pineapple and coleslaw mix. Season with salt and pepper to taste, if desired.

Makes 4 to 6 servings

Creamy Filled Brownies

- ½ **cup (1 stick) butter or margarine**
- ⅓ **cup HERSHEY'S Cocoa**
- 2 **eggs**
- 1 **cup sugar**
- ½ **cup all-purpose flour**
- ¼ **teaspoon baking powder**
- ¼ **teaspoon salt**
- 1 **teaspoon vanilla extract**
- 1 **cup finely chopped nuts**
- **Creamy Filling (recipe follows)**
- **Mini Chip Glaze (recipe follows)**
- ½ **cup sliced almonds or chopped nuts (optional)**

1. Heat oven to 350°F. Line 15½×10½×1-inch jelly roll pan with foil; grease foil.

2. Melt butter in small saucepan; remove from heat. Stir in cocoa until smooth. Beat eggs in medium bowl; gradually add sugar, beating until fluffy. Stir together flour, baking powder and salt; add to egg mixture. Add cocoa mixture and vanilla; beat well. Stir in chopped nuts. Spread batter in prepared pan.

3. Bake 12 to 14 minutes or until top springs back when touched lightly in center. Cool completely in pan on wire rack; remove from pan to cutting board. Remove foil; cut brownie in half crosswise. Spread one half with Creamy Filling; top with second half. Spread Mini Chip Glaze over top; sprinkle with sliced almonds, if desired. After glaze has set, cut into bars.   *Makes about 24 brownies*

Creamy Filling: Beat 1 package (3 ounces) softened cream cheese, 2 tablespoons softened butter or margarine and 1 teaspoon vanilla extract in small bowl. Gradually add 1½ cups powdered sugar, beating until of spreading consistency.

Mini Chip Glaze: Heat ¼ cup sugar and 2 tablespoons water to boiling in small saucepan. Remove from heat. Immediately add ½ cup HERSHEY'S MINI CHIPS™ Semi-Sweet Chocolate Chips, stirring until melted.

Roasted Turkey Breast with Cherry & Apple Rice Stuffing

3³/4 cups water
3 boxes UNCLE BEN'S® Long Grain & Wild Rice Butter & Herb Fast Cook Recipe
¹/2 cup butter or margarine, divided
¹/2 cup dried red tart cherries
1 large apple, peeled and chopped (about 1 cup)
¹/2 cup sliced almonds, toasted*
1 bone-in turkey breast (5 to 6 pounds)

*To toast almonds, place them on a baking sheet. Bake 10 to 12 minutes in preheated 325°F oven or until golden brown, stirring occasionally.

1. In large saucepan, combine water, rice, contents of seasoning packets, 3 tablespoons butter and cherries. Bring to a boil. Cover; reduce heat to low and simmer 25 minutes or until all water is absorbed. Stir in apple and almonds; set aside.

2. Preheat oven to 325°F. Place turkey breast, skin side down, on rack in roasting pan. Loosely fill breast cavity with rice stuffing. (Place any remaining stuffing in greased baking dish; cover and refrigerate. Bake alongside turkey for 35 to 40 minutes or until heated through.)

3. Place sheet of heavy-duty foil over stuffing, molding it slightly over sides of turkey. Carefully invert turkey, skin side up, on rack. Melt remaining 5 tablespoons butter; brush some of butter over surface of turkey.

4. Roast turkey, uncovered, 1 hour; baste with melted butter. Continue roasting 1¹/4 to 1³/4 hours, basting occasionally with melted butter, until meat thermometer inserted into center of thickest part of turkey breast, not touching bone, registers 170°F. Let turkey stand, covered, 15 minutes before carving.

Makes 6 to 8 servings

Strawberry Cheesecake Pie

1 *prepared* 9-inch (6 ounces) graham cracker crumb crust

⅔ cup (5 fluid-ounce can) NESTLÉ® CARNATION® Evaporated Fat Free Milk

1 package (8 ounces) fat-free cream cheese, softened

1 large egg

...ar, flour and lemon
... into crust.

... Cool completely
... of pie; drizzle

Makes 8 servings

Green Beans
with Toasted Pecans

  **3 tablespoons I CAN'T BELIEVE IT'S NOT BUTTER!® Spread,
  melted**
  1 teaspoon sugar
  ¼ teaspoon garlic powder
    Pinch ground red pepper
    Salt to taste
  ⅓ cup chopped pecans
  1 pound green beans

In small bowl, blend I Can't Believe It's Not Butter!® Spread, sugar, garlic powder, pepper and salt. In 12-inch nonstick skillet, heat 2 teaspoons garlic mixture over medium-high heat; cook pecans, stirring frequently, 2 minutes or until pecans are golden. Remove pecans; set aside. In same skillet, heat remaining garlic mixture and stir in green beans. Cook, covered, over medium heat, stirring occasionally, 6 minutes or until green beans are tender. Stir in pecans.
Makes 4 servings

Honey-Glazed Carrots

  3 cups sliced carrots
  6 tablespoons honey
  2 tablespoons *each* butter and chopped fresh parsley
  1½ teaspoons Dijon mustard

Bring 1 cup of salted water to a boil in saucepan over high heat. Add carrots; return to a boil. Reduce heat to medium. Cover; cook 8 to 12 minutes or until crisp-tender. Drain water. Stir in honey, butter, parsley and mustard. Cook and stir over low heat until carrots are glazed.
Makes 6 servings

Favorite recipe from **National Honey Board**

Peanut Butter Kisses

  1 cup granulated sugar
  1 cup packed brown sugar
  1 cup CRISCO® all-vegetable shortening
  1 cup JIF® Peanut Butter
  2 eggs
  ¼ cup milk
  2 teaspoons vanilla
  3½ cups sifted all-purpose flour
  2 teaspoons baking soda
  1 teaspoon salt
  1 (11-ounce) package milk chocolate candies

1. Heat oven to 375°F.

2. Cream together granulated sugar, brown sugar, shortening and peanut butter. Add eggs, milk and vanilla; beat well.

3. Stir together flour, baking soda and salt; add to peanut butter mixture. Beat well.

4. Shape dough into 1-inch balls; roll in additional granulated sugar. Place on ungreased cookie sheet.

5. Bake at 375°F for 8 minutes. Remove from oven. Press one milk chocolate candy into center of each warm cookie.

6. Return to oven; bake 3 minutes longer.

Makes 6 to 7 dozen cookies

Ragú® Chili Mac

1 tablespoon olive oil
1 medium green bell pepper, chopped
1 pound ground beef
1 jar (1 pound 10 ounces) RAGÚ® Old World Style® Pasta Sauce
2 tablespoons chili powder
8 ounces elbow macaroni, cooked and drained

1. In 12-inch nonstick skillet, heat olive oil over medium-high heat and cook green bell pepper, stirring occasionally, 3 minutes. Add ground beef and brown, stirring occasionally; drain.

2. Stir in Ragú Pasta Sauce and chili powder. Bring to a boil over high heat. Reduce heat to low and simmer covered 10 minutes.

3. Stir in macaroni and heat through. Serve, if desired, with sour cream and shredded Cheddar cheese.   *Makes 4 servings*

Prep Time: 10 minutes
Cook Time: 25 minutes

Salsa Macaroni & Cheese

1 jar (1 pound) RAGÚ® Cheese Creations!® Double Cheddar Sauce
1 cup prepared mild salsa
8 ounces elbow macaroni, cooked and drained

1. In 2-quart saucepan, heat Ragú Cheese Creations! Sauce over medium heat. Stir in salsa; heat through.

2. Toss with hot macaroni. Serve immediately.

Makes 4 servings

Buttermilk Ranch Fried Chicken

2½ to 3 pounds fryer chicken pieces
   WESSON® Vegetable Oil
2¼ cups all-purpose flour
1¼ tablespoons dried dill weed
1½ teaspoons salt
   ¾ teaspoon pepper
2½ cups buttermilk

Rinse chicken and pat dry; set aside. Fill a large deep-fry pot or electric skillet to no more than half its depth with Wesson® Oil. Heat oil to 325°F to 350°F. In a medium bowl, combine flour, dill, salt and pepper. Fill another bowl with buttermilk. Place chicken, one piece at a time, in buttermilk; shake off excess liquid. Coat lightly in flour mixture; shake off excess flour. Dip once again in buttermilk and flour mixture. Fry chicken, a few pieces at a time, skin side down, for 10 to 14 minutes. Turn chicken and fry 12 to 15 minutes longer or until juices run clear; drain on paper towels. Let stand 7 minutes before serving.   *Makes 4 servings*

Cook's Tip: To reduce frying time by 7 to 9 minutes per side, simply cook unbreaded chicken in boiling water for 15 minutes; remove and cool completely before proceeding with recipe.

Italian-Style Meat Loaf

1 egg
1½ pounds lean ground beef or turkey
8 ounces hot or mild Italian sausage, casings removed
1 cup CONTADINA® Seasoned Bread Crumbs
1 can (8 ounces) CONTADINA Tomato Sauce, divided
1 cup finely chopped onion
½ cup finely chopped green bell pepper

1. Beat egg lightly in large bowl. Add beef, sausage, bread crumbs, ¾ cup tomato sauce, onion and bell pepper; mix well.

2. Press into ungreased 9×5-inch loaf pan. Bake, uncovered, in preheated 350°F oven for 60 minutes.

3. Spoon remaining tomato sauce over meat loaf. Bake 15 minutes longer or until no longer pink in center; drain. Let stand for 10 minutes before serving. *Makes 8 servings*

Prep Time: 10 minutes
Cook Time: 75 minutes
Standing Time: 10 minutes

Bittersweet Pecan Brownies with Caramel Sauce

Brownies
- ¾ **cup all-purpose flour**
- ¼ **teaspoon baking soda**
- **4 squares (1 ounce each) bittersweet or unsweetened chocolate, coarsely chopped**
- ½ **cup (1 stick) plus 2 tablespoons I CAN'T BELIEVE IT'S NOT BUTTER!® Spread**
- ¾ **cup granulated sugar**
- **2 eggs**
- ½ **cup chopped pecans**

Caramel Sauce
- ¾ **cup firmly packed light brown sugar**
- **6 tablespoons I CAN'T BELIEVE IT'S NOT BUTTER!® Spread**
- ⅓ **cup whipping or heavy cream**
- ½ **teaspoon apple cider vinegar or fresh lemon juice**

For brownies, preheat oven to 325°F. Line 8-inch square baking pan with aluminum foil, then grease and flour foil; set aside.

In small bowl, combine flour and baking soda; set aside. In medium microwave-safe bowl, microwave chocolate and I Can't Believe It's Not Butter!® Spread at HIGH (Full Power) 1 minute or until chocolate is melted; stir until smooth. With wooden spoon, beat in granulated sugar, then eggs. Beat in flour mixture. Evenly spread into prepared pan; sprinkle with pecans. Bake 31 minutes or until toothpick inserted in center comes out clean. On wire rack, cool completely; remove brownies by lifting edges of foil. Cut brownies into 4 squares, then cut each square into 2 triangles.

For caramel sauce, in medium saucepan, bring brown sugar, I Can't Believe It's Not Butter! Spread and cream just to a boil over high heat, stirring frequently. Cook 3 minutes. Stir in vinegar. To serve, pour caramel sauce around brownie and top, if desired, with vanilla or caramel ice cream.   *Makes 8 servings*

Lasagna Supreme

  8 ounces uncooked lasagna noodles
½ pound ground beef
½ pound mild Italian sausage, casings removed
  1 medium onion, chopped
  2 cloves garlic, minced
  1 can (14½ ounces) diced tomatoes, undrained
  1 can (6 ounces) tomato paste
  2 teaspoons dried basil leaves
  1 teaspoon dried marjoram leaves
  1 can (4 ounces) sliced mushrooms, drained
  2 eggs
  2 cups (16 ounces) cream-style cottage cheese
¾ cup grated Parmesan cheese, divided
  2 tablespoons dried parsley flakes
½ teaspoon salt
½ teaspoon black pepper
  2 cups (8 ounces) shredded Cheddar cheese
  3 cups (12 ounces) shredded mozzarella cheese

1. Cook lasagna noodles according to package directions; drain.

2. Cook meats, onion and garlic in large skillet over medium-high heat until meat is brown, stirring to separate meat. Drain drippings from skillet. Add tomatoes with juice, tomato paste, basil and marjoram. Reduce heat to low. Cover; simmer 15 minutes, stirring often. Stir in mushrooms; set aside.

3. Preheat oven to 375°F. Beat eggs in large bowl; add cottage cheese, ½ cup Parmesan cheese, parsley, salt and pepper. Mix well.

4. Place half the noodles in bottom of greased 13×9-inch baking pan. Spread half the cottage cheese mixture over noodles, then half the meat mixture and half the Cheddar cheese and mozzarella cheese. Repeat layers. Sprinkle with remaining ¼ cup Parmesan cheese. Bake lasagna 40 to 45 minutes or until bubbly. Let stand 10 minutes before cutting. *Makes 8 to 10 servings*

Hearty Chicken and Rice Soup

    10 cups chicken broth
     1 medium onion, chopped
     1 cup sliced celery
     1 cup sliced carrots
    ¼ cup snipped fresh parsley
    ½ teaspoon cracked black pepper
    ½ teaspoon dried thyme leaves
     1 bay leaf
  1½ cups cubed chicken (about ¾ pound)
     2 cups cooked rice
     2 tablespoons lime juice
       Lime slices for garnish

Combine broth, onion, celery, carrots, parsley, pepper, thyme and bay leaf in Dutch oven. Bring to a boil, stirring once or twice. Reduce heat; simmer, uncovered, 10 to 15 minutes. Add chicken; simmer, uncovered, 5 to 10 minutes or until chicken is no longer pink in center. Remove and discard bay leaf. Stir in rice and lime juice just before serving. Garnish with lime slices.

Makes 8 servings

Favorite recipe from **USA Rice Federation**

Banana Boat Sundae

HERSHEY'S Special Dark® Syrup
3 scoops vanilla ice cream
1 banana, peeled and sliced in half lengthwise
REESE'S® Shell Topping®
HERSHEY'S Classic Caramel™ Sundae Syrup
HERSHEY'S Chocolate Shoppe™ Milk Chocolate Sprinkles
HERSHEY'S Double Chocolate Sundae Syrup
REDDI-WIP® Whipped Topping

• Pour layer of HERSHEY'S Special Dark Syrup into banana split sundae dish.

• Place 3 scoops of ice cream next to each other on top of syrup. Place banana half on both sides of ice cream scoops.

• Top first ice cream scoop with REESE'S Shell Topping. Top second scoop with HERSHEY'S Classic Caramel Sundae Syrup and HERSHEY'S Chocolate Shoppe Milk Chocolate Sprinkles. Top third scoop with HERSHEY'S Double Chocolate Sundae Syrup. Top with REDDI-WIP Whipped Topping.   *Makes 1 sundae*

Potatoes au Gratin

4 to 6 medium unpeeled baking potatoes (about 2 pounds)
2 cups (8 ounces) shredded Cheddar cheese
1 cup (4 ounces) shredded Swiss cheese
2 tablespoons butter or margarine
3 tablespoons all-purpose flour
2½ cups milk
2 tablespoons Dijon mustard
¼ teaspoon salt
¼ teaspoon black pepper

1. Preheat oven to 400°F. Grease 13×9-inch baking dish.

2. Cut potatoes into thin slices. Layer potatoes in prepared dish. Top with cheeses.

3. Melt butter in medium saucepan over medium heat. Stir in flour; cook 1 minute. Stir in milk, mustard, salt and pepper; bring to a boil. Reduce heat and cook, stirring constantly, until mixture thickens. Pour milk mixture over cheese. Cover pan with foil.

4. Bake 30 minutes. Remove foil and bake 15 to 20 minutes or until potatoes are tender and top is brown. Remove from oven; let stand 10 minutes before serving.   *Makes 6 to 8 servings*

Butter Toffee Chocolate Chip Crunch

1 cup firmly packed light brown sugar

¾ Butter Flavor CRISCO® stick or ¾ cup Butter Flavor CRISCO® all-vegetable shortening plus additional for greasing

1 egg

2 tablespoons sweetened condensed milk (not evaporated milk)

1 teaspoon salt

¾ teaspoon baking soda

1 teaspoon vanilla

1¾ cups all-purpose flour

¾ cup coarsely chopped pecans

½ cup milk chocolate chips

½ cup semisweet chocolate chips

2 to 4 bars (1.4 ounces each) toffee bars, finely crushed

1. Heat oven to 350°F. Grease baking sheet with shortening. Place sheets of foil on countertop for cooling cookies.

2. Combine brown sugar, shortening, egg, sweetened condensed milk, salt, baking soda and vanilla in large bowl. Beat at medium speed of electric mixer until well blended. Add flour gradually at low speed. Beat until well blended. Stir in nuts, milk chocolate chips, semisweet chocolate chips and crushed toffee bars with spoon. Drop by level measuring tablespoonfuls 2 inches apart onto prepared baking sheet.

3. Bake at 350°F for 10 to 12 minutes or until light golden brown. *Do not overbake.* Cool 2 minutes on baking sheet. Remove cookies to foil to cool completely.   *Makes about 4 dozen cookies*

Lemon Bars

Crust
>   2 cups all-purpose flour
>   ½ cup powdered sugar
>   1 cup (2 sticks) butter or margarine, softened

Filling
>   1 can (14 ounces) NESTLÉ® CARNATION® Sweetened
>   Condensed Milk
>   4 large eggs
>   ⅔ cup lemon juice
>   1 tablespoon all-purpose flour
>   1 teaspoon baking powder
>   ¼ teaspoon salt
>   4 drops yellow food coloring (optional)
>   1 tablespoon grated lemon peel
>   Sifted powdered sugar (optional)

PREHEAT oven to 350°F.

For Crust

COMBINE flour and sugar in medium bowl. Cut in butter with pastry blender or two knives until mixture is crumbly. Press lightly onto bottom and halfway up sides of ungreased 13×9-inch baking pan.

BAKE for 20 minutes.

For Filling

BEAT sweetened condensed milk and eggs in large mixer bowl until fluffy. Beat in lemon juice, flour, baking powder, salt and food coloring just until blended. Fold in lemon peel; pour over crust.

BAKE for 20 to 25 minutes or until filling is set and crust is golden brown. Cool in pan on wire rack. Refrigerate for about 2 hours. Cut into bars; sprinkle with powdered sugar.   *Makes 4 dozen bars*

Acknowledgments

The publisher would like to thank the companies
and organizations listed below for the use of their recipes
and photographs in this publication.

Crisco is a registered trademark of
The J.M. Smucker Company

Del Monte Corporation

Hershey Foods Corporation

Kraft Foods Holdings

MASTERFOODS USA

National Honey Board

Nestlé USA

Reddi-wip® and WESSON® Oil are registered trademarks of
ConAgra Brands, Inc.

Unilever Foods North America

USA Rice Federation